W9-CDX-522

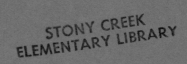

Rio Grande

RIO GRANDE

FROM THE ROCKY MOUNTAINS TO THE GULF OF MEXICO

PETER LOURIE

BOYDS MILLS PRESS

RIO GRANDE RIVER

◆ ◆ ◆

After seeing the Rio Grande for the first time, the humorist Will Rogers remarked that it was the only river he had seen in need of irrigation.

CONTENTS

P R O L O G U E

◆　　　◆　　　◆

At 12,000 feet in the rugged San Juan Mountains of Southern Colorado, five creeks come together to form the source of the third longest river in the United States—the Rio Grande, Spanish for "Great River." From its headwaters in the Rocky Mountains, the *Río Bravo del Norte*, the "Swift River of the North," as the Spaniards called it, flows over rapids down the spruce- and aspen-studded slopes of the Rockies, home of the bighorn sheep, elk, and black bear.

Flowing south, the river leaves Colorado and runs through the center of New Mexico, ancient land of the Pueblo and the first Spanish settlers. At El Paso, Texas, the Rio Grande turns to the southeast where it flows through desert and forms a 1,000-mile river border between the United States and Mexico. Finally, 1,885

miles from its Rocky Mountain source on the Continental Divide, diminished by irrigation and evaporation, the Rio Grande ends its long journey as it flows gently into the Gulf of Mexico.

Most great North American rivers, like the Mississippi, the Ohio, the Hudson, and even the Missouri with its shifting sand bars, have been commercial waterways for tugs and barges and steamboats. But not the Rio Grande. This shallow, bony river remains unpredictable. Some years certain portions dry up. Unlike many rivers, the Rio Grande is fed by few major tributaries. Yet the Great River travels nearly two thousand miles through mountains and deserts, all the way to the salt water of the Gulf. One summer I discovered what makes the Rio Grande so grand.

CHAPTER ONE

◆ ◆ ◆

HEADWATERS

THE CONTINENTAL DIVIDE

In July I drove through the Rockies to the Continental Divide, a ridge in the mountains separating rivers flowing to different sides of the continent. Water on the western slope of the divide drains toward the Colorado River and the Pacific Ocean. Water on the eastern side drains into the Rio Grande, which feeds the Gulf of Mexico.

In the snow-capped mountains, I found the headwaters of the Rio Grande. Nearly two thousand miles from the sea, the river is a clear mountain stream full of rainbow and brown trout. Before the miners came in the late 1800s, this was the hunting ground of the Ute Indians. I stayed in a log cabin on a ranch that had been homesteaded since 1882. The night was cold and crisp. As I watched the moon grow big in the sky, I fell in love with the land and the sound of the murmuring river as it moved swiftly by the cabin.

9

This old silver mine is a ghostly reminder of the boom days.

Creede today.
(opposite page) Creede in days gone by: a Wild West town.

CREEDE

A few miles downriver from the ranch, I came to Creede, the first town on the Rio Grande. Built at the end of a canyon that leads up to the silver mines, Creede was founded in the mining boom days of the 1890s. Silver continued to be mined here until 1985, when the last silver mine shut down.

On the steep hills behind Creede I saw the rubble of old mines, forgotten tunnels, mills, and tailing piles, and the dark wooden ribs of tumbledown cabins. These were the ghostly remains of abandoned diggings. I could picture the burros of the prospectors. I could almost hear the mountain silence shattered by the sounds of hammers and picks and mule teams and heavy ore crashing down the mountain canyon to the mill.

But now the wind was all I heard. There was a sadness in the still, bright air, the sadness of time passed and time passing.

Jesse James robbed banks and trains from Arkansas to Texas. His exploits made him a legend in his time. His fame grew larger after Bob Ford shot him in 1882.

Frank James, Jesse's brother and fellow outlaw.

The infamous Bob Ford.

In the town's historical museum I found newspaper clippings from the wild days of Creede:

Sunday night was marked with more disorder than any previous one in the camp's history. Bob Ford and Joe Palmer got on a raid and shot Jimtown [Creede's former name] full of holes. Buildings were perforated, and window panes broken and the air badly cracked up with pistol balls. Not an officer was to be seen ... It lasted from eight o'clock till twelve o'clock, when the ammunition ran out.

—The Creede Candle, April 29, 1892

Creede had been a lawless gulch. Mining sharks, saloon keepers, pickpockets, dance hall girls, and professional gamblers made up half the population. The town attracted such well-known figures as Calamity Jane, Soapy Smith, and Bat Masterson.

Perhaps the most notorious resident of Creede was Bob Ford, the man who shot the outlaw Jesse James. After he killed Jesse in Missouri, Bob Ford drifted into Creede and opened a saloon. Ford tried to run the town, but the people of Creede hated the "baby-faced killer of Jesse James." Jesse's brother Frank came to Creede to avenge his brother's death. But he was too late. The day before Frank got to town, Ford was gunned down in his own saloon.

(Right) The town turned out to bid farewell to Bob Ford (coffin on wagon in center). Look closely and you can see "Bob Ford's Dance Hall."

Down the river with "Mountain Man."

MOUNTAIN MAN

I met "Mountain Man" Greg Coln on one of his Rio Grande rafting trips. As a boy in Tennessee, Greg canoed many rivers. Today he is a happy and free river guide. Years ago he had given up a high-paying job in Texas so he could live alone in the Rocky Mountains.

"That job, by some people's standards, was a pretty successful one. But I just wasn't happy," he said. So one day "Mountain Man" loaded up his backpack, left Texas, and arrived in these mountains with a black-powder rifle and a black-powder pistol, just like the mountain men of old. He found an old trapper's cabin fifteen miles from Creede. He packed in a few supplies before the first snows fell. The snow covered his cabin, and he had to dig his way out. He spent the year alone. When Greg appeared for supplies, people said, "Oh, here comes that crazy mountain man!"

A family from Texas joined us when we put the raft into the Rio Grande at Wagon Wheel Gap. It was a sunny afternoon, the sky a deep blue. Creede has one of the most beautiful stretches of the Rio Grande. No boats with motors are allowed on the upper river. Here the river is free of pollution. The water is clear and fast, and more green than brown.

The whitewater was fun and not too scary. Greg laughed as he rowed us around the rocks. Sometimes he takes his kayak to run the upper Rio Grande by moonlight. "You can hear the rapids ahead. Then suddenly you see them in the magic light of the full moon!"

Storm clouds had formed as we ended our trip, but now and then rays of sun pierced through the pearl of the sky. We pulled the raft out of the river, and I said goodbye to "Mountain Man." I smelled wild roses and ponderosa in the hills and marveled at the snowcapped mountains. This was indeed a great beginning for a my river journey.

CHAPTER TWO

◆　◆　◆

PUEBLOS

A WAY OF LIFE

I left the mountains behind me, driving south through the fertile San Luis Valley, passing towns with Spanish names such as Alamosa, Del Norte, and Monte Vista. I crossed over the Colorado border into New Mexico.

Here the river straightens its course, and the mountains recede into the distance. In the wide, open river valley, yellow and red and blue flowers bloomed in the arid soil. Multiple rainbows formed over the hills. The sage-filled air made this part of the river perhaps the most enchanted of all.

In New Mexico, the Rio Grande passes through the ancient land of the Pueblo people. *Pueblo* means "village" in Spanish. The Spaniards who came up the Rio Grande Valley in 1540 called its inhabitants Pueblos because the people lived

The Taos Pueblo, stark and beautiful under the desert sun.

in permanent villages instead of the temporary shelters of nomadic tribes like the Comanche and the Apache. The Pueblo people have been living in villages throughout the desert of the Southwest for two thousand years, and their hunter-gatherer ancestors roamed the area for ten thousand years before that.

The early Spanish expedition led by Francisco Vásquez de Coronado was searching the area for gold. The Spaniards found the Pueblo people farming beans, corn, and squash. Because the Pueblos had no gold, they were never destroyed

Water is precious, and for ages the river has been a great provider. This photo from 1883 shows the San Felipe Pueblo as viewed from across the Rio Grande.

as a people, unlike the Incas in South America. The Pueblo people still practice many traditional ways of their ancestors.

There are nineteen distinct Pueblos in New Mexico today. Each has its own government, customs, ceremonies, and traditions. Although diverse, these people share a common culture. Their dwellings are made from the materials of the land—stone, clay, and mud—and the houses look much like natural outcrops of the land itself. Villages are clusters of box-shaped dwellings often piled stories high. Ladders connect the levels and can be pulled up in times of danger.

The clusters of individual houses are often built around open-air spaces called plazas, areas used for dances and religious ceremonies of the tribe. Until modern times, each Pueblo survived primarily by agriculture. Now the Pueblo people have modern conveniences. Although many live and work off the reservation, the Pueblo people still identify with their Pueblos and return for ceremonial events.

But some fear the Pueblo way of life may be threatened, as the health of the river is in peril. Developers have built so many homes that the water in the Rio Grande is being sucked out at alarming rates. The Pueblos are worried about the dropping water table. They depend on the water for their crops. Water is the number one resource in this area, not gold!

PETROGLYPHS

Just north of the San Juan Pueblo, a local man told me how to reach some boulders with ancient petroglyphs on them.

Petroglyphs near the San Juan Pueblo.

(opposite page) Puyé ruins on the mesa.

It was a beautiful but very hot day when I climbed the hill along the shore. Looking over the plains of the Rio Grande, I found mysterious drawings everywhere—circles and symbols, animal and human figures. Petroglyphs are pecked or abraded marks that native peoples long ago made on rocks, boulders, cliff sides, and other stone outcroppings. Often formed by hitting or grinding the rock with a tool, petroglyphs are lighter than the rock they are carved into. This is because the rocks accumulate a kind of natural dark varnish over time. When a petroglyph is chiseled into the dark stone, the petroglyph itself exposes the lighter-colored interior of the rock.

Why did these ancient people draw petroglyphs, I wondered. Archeologists believe that some petroglyphs must have marked a trail or showed the place to find water. Ceremonies might have been performed near the petroglyphs. Some surely were observations of the stars, the sun, and the moon. Others are clear representations of people or animals or stories. Still others baffle modern observers.

PUYÉ RUINS

I also explored the ancient Pueblo village at Puyé. Located on a mesa top in the reservation of the Santa Clara Pueblo, Puyé was inhabited from about 1250 to 1580 A.D. More than a thousand Pueblos lived here for three centuries, but had had to abandon the site when drought and failing crops forced them to leave. As I walked through Puyé I imagined children playing and laughing on the mesa centuries ago. No echoes of

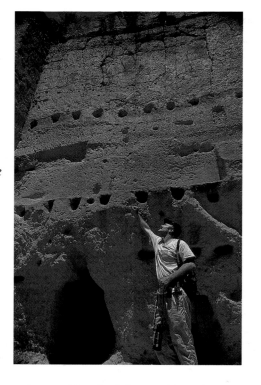

In winter the people of Puyé came down from the mesa and lived in caves. Ancient symbols are carved above the caves.

A mesa in the enchanted land of the Pueblo.

their laughter remained. Yet something about the abandoned village seemed sacred in its silence. The earth was dry and dusty. The small rooms were made from shaped blocks of volcanic tuff quarried from the edges of the mesa top. The ruins looked orange in the late day sun.

Here, too, I found the village *kiva*. *Kiva* is a Hopi word meaning "ceremonial chamber." It is where the spiritual activity of the Pueblo once took place. Some modern kivas are above ground, but the Puyé kiva consisted of a chamber inside the earth reached by descending a thick wooden ladder. I descended into the cool room with a sense of respect and fear. The floor was packed earth. Along the edge of the round space was a bench cut in stone. I tried to imagine the sacred gatherings that took place here over the centuries.

CORN DANCE AT COCHITI PUEBLO

For the Pueblos, the Rio Grande is the great provider. I was fortunate to be on the river for the annual feast day and corn dance of the Cochiti Pueblo. This is the most important feast day of the year. The songs and dances at the corn festival call for clouds to bring rain, crops to grow, and people to prosper.

When I reached the Pueblo, the first thing I spotted when I got out of my car was one of many signs that read: ABSOLUTELY NO CAMERAS, NO TAPE RECORDERS, NO VIDEOS, NO SKETCHING.

In every Pueblo along the Rio Grande, I found the same signs warning tourists not to take photos. So much has been stolen from the Pueblo people since the Europeans first arrived

This is the plaza where I witnessed the annual corn dance. The Cochiti Pueblo looks much as it did in 1901, the year this photograph was taken.

that today they are extremely protective of what they have left, such as their religious festivals. Too often photographs and recordings have been made and then used to sell products. Often the photographs are mislabeled, and the seriousness of Pueblo traditions has been cheapened.

I respected the Pueblo's wishes and left my tape recorder and cameras in the car. I understood that it is because of this very vigilance that the Pueblo people still speak their own language. They remember the old ways. The dances and songs are still alive.

I was happy that the Cochiti people graciously allowed outsiders like me to view the most important festival of the year. The day was hotter than normal, perhaps 98 degrees. In the plaza at the center of the village, more than two hundred dancers in traditional dress danced their majestic steps, forming lines around a drummer, who beat a steady haunting beat.

In the middle of the dancers was the choir, which consisted of fifty older men in bold-colored shirts. The choir stood near the drummer and turned slowly in unison to face all directions of the compass as the men sang their ancient songs.

Then the "turquoise people," those with skin painted blue, came out and danced. They circled the plaza in a long line and divided up into two rows. Next came the "pumpkin people," their faces and arms red. The men held rattles in one hand and Douglas fir branches in the other. The women wore black dresses and white moccasins and held fir branches in each palm as if offering them to the sky. Male dancers wore bells and shells and sometimes a fox pelt.

The rhythms of the bells, the delicate stamping of hundreds of feet in the dry white dust, the serious faces of the Cochiti dancers, the smell of the dancers' bodies, pungent and now mixing with the smoke from fires and the dust itself—all this, hour after hour, seemed like a dream or a trance.

I felt transported outside of time to a place of eternal ritual.

Pat Garrett and Billy the Kid.

BILLY THE KID

Leaving the Cochiti Pueblo behind, I drove south of Albuquerque where the Rio Grande struggles through a stark desert of cactus, mesquite, and yucca. The Rio Grande is such a major source of water for cattle and crops that one year too much water was diverted from this section of the river, and it all but dried up. In 1993 the Rio Grande was declared one of America's most endangered rivers.

Before leaving New Mexico, I explored the territory of the famous outlaw Billy the Kid. The Kid rarely drank alcohol, and he didn't smoke. He did, however, have a hot temper, and he loved to dance with the *señoritas*. His real name was Henry McCarty, although some say it might have been William Bonney. His place and date of birth are a mystery, but many think he was born in New York City. As a boy he loved to listen to music and read books. After his mother died, he ran afoul of the law and started rustling cattle in New Mexico. Then he killed a blacksmith and fled.

Across the Rio Grande from the city of Las Cruces, the little town of Mesilla, New Mexico, was an overnight stop in the days of the stagecoach. Many outlaws and rustlers like Billy the Kid wandered through Mesilla. In 1881 Billy the Kid was tried here for the murder of a lawman. The old Mesilla courthouse stands on the plaza even today.

The Kid was sentenced to hang, but he escaped. That same year Billy the Kid was hunted down and shot by Sheriff Pat Garrett, another legendary figure of the Southwest.

CHAPTER THREE

◆ ◆ ◆

THE BORDER

TEXAS & MEXICO

When it reaches El Paso, Texas, the Rio Grande becomes a border between Mexico and the United States for the rest of its 1000-mile course to the Gulf of Mexico. Texas towns along the border tend to be influenced by Mexican culture. In many towns eight out of every ten residents are of Mexican descent.

Until 1836 Texas was part of Mexico. But fiercely independent and increasingly populated by Anglo settlers, Texas had deep cultural and commercial ties with the United States. War broke out between the defiant American settlers and the Mexican government in 1835. And in 1836 the Mexican army, led by General Antonio López de Santa Anna, crossed the Rio Grande from the south to quell the rebellion. This led to the famous defense of the Alamo.

General Santa Anna

General Sam Houston

Defending the mission, nearly two hundred Americans commanded by William Travis and including Davy Crockett and Jim Bowie, fought valiantly against thousands of Mexican troops but eventually succumbed to the greater force. Six weeks later, however, General Santa Anna was defeated by General Sam Houston's forces. On the afternoon of April 21, 1836, at San Jacinto, the Texans attacked during the Mexican army's siesta. Their battle cry was "Remember the Alamo." General Santa Anna fled but was later captured and imprisoned for six months. Texas had achieved independence from Mexico.

Texas remained an independent state until it joined the Union in 1845, becoming the 28th state, which led to the two-year Mexican-American War. When Mexican forces finally retreated south of the Rio Grande, more settlers from the north poured into Texas to grow cotton and raise cattle. The U.S. victory over Mexico established the Rio Grande as the border between the two countries. Mexico had lost over half of its territory, including present-day California, New Mexico, and northern Arizona.

Across the Rio Grande today in some Mexican towns there is no running water, and jobs can pay as little as seventy-five cents a day. But when I crossed the bridge at El Paso into Juárez, Mexico, I found music and laughter in the streets.

BORDER PATROL

I walked many times across the bridge from El Paso into Juárez. One day I looked below and saw a group of six people

Crossing from Mexico into Texas.

wading across the river from the Mexican side with their clothes in plastic bags held high over their heads. They stopped when they saw a U. S. Border Patrol agent on a bike watching them from the bridge. Slowly they retreated to shore. I supposed they would attempt to cross later.

Trying to stop illegal crossings is like trying to hold a fistful of sand. The border is like a sieve.

The U.S. Border Patrol, a law enforcement arm of the Justice Department, has been assigned the difficult job of surveying the border and catching anyone trying to cross into the United States illegally. Often the Border Patrol captures people trying to smuggle drugs across the border.

The U. S. Border Patrol (Circa 1919).

Most people from Mexico, however, cross the border legally to work. They look at the United States as a place to earn a decent living. Thousands apply for legal immigrant status, but many are denied, so they slip across the border to find jobs. Often these are men whose families remain in Mexico, and the money they make is sent home.

The problem of illegal crossings is a source of conflict for the two countries. Daily, thousands are turned back to Mexico, yet thousands try again to slip across the border.

HEADING FOR THE RIVER

During the early part of the century, the Border Patrol did much of their surveillance on horseback. In many areas there were

A day's catch from the Rio Grande.

no roads at all. Even today a few horse patrol agents ride by night along the border looking for people sneaking across the river.

I went to the main office of the El Paso sector of the U.S. Border Patrol, which covers 109 miles of the Texas river border with Mexico. There I met Agent Linda Hochule, who agreed to take me to the border. The job can be dangerous. Agents had been fired on several times in the past three weeks from the Mexican side of the border.

Agent Hochule is one of only forty-five women out of the one thousand agents in this sector. She speaks fluent Spanish. She was scared, she said, when she first started her job, especially when she worked alone at night.

We headed for the river in an unmarked, four-wheel-drive Suburban. The temperature was 105 degrees. The sun glared like a knife to the eyes. Agent Hochule got out and walked along the Rio Grande, which was only twenty yards wide. She peered into the brushy areas, and kept her hand on her pistol at all times. She looked for footprints.

A child from the Mexican side of the river showed Agent Hochule a catfish he had just caught. But I could tell her presence made him nervous, and I felt sad about the tensions along our border with his country.

Pancho Villa

CHAPTER FOUR

◆ ◆ ◆

BIG BEND

THE UNINHABITABLE LAND

Now, remarkably, the river flows southeast on the edge of the great Mexican Chihuahuan desert. Then it turns east and even northeast as it literally bends in a triangle through the dramatic and relatively unknown canyons and mountains of Big Bend National Park. Here I left the car to raft twenty-one miles of the wild and scenic river.

Big Bend is one of the Rio Grande's great secrets. This is the badlands of the Southwest. Spaniards called it *El Despoblado*, or "the uninhabited place." Native American legend says this was where the Great Spirit deposited all the leftover rocks after creating the earth. It is off the beaten path of most tourists, but its treasures are many. The river, the desert plain, and the mountains offer wild scenery unlike anywhere else in the country. Ghost towns still haunt the desert, and some

33

A man with a rowboat gave me a ride into Mexico.

I made new friends in the village.

locals say tons of Spanish gold and silver lie buried in the rugged mountains of the Big Bend.

I spent a night at Lajitas on the Rio Grande, a former U.S. Cavalry post. The famous Mexican revolutionary Pancho Villa and his men roamed through this area in the early 1900s, often crossing the Rio Grande. A rebel against social abuses, Villa was famous for his horsemanship. His daring raids along the river made him a sort of Robin Hood to the masses of northern Mexico.

For thousands of years, too, the river at Lajitas with its smooth rock bottom was known as the best river crossing between the points of Del Rio and El Paso. The Comanche crossed here on seasonal migrations and raids.

MEXICO

Unlike in El Paso, along most of the Rio Grande border there is no obvious sign of the Border Patrol. One can pass back and forth freely as if it were all one land. But the two countries are in fact very different. Mexico is a country of opposites. The rich live alongside the poor. Some resources seem unlimited; others, like forests, are quickly disappearing under a population explosion. The country is filled with young people. One out of every three Mexicans is under the age of fifteen.

Crossing the Rio Grande was like crossing into a former century, a simpler existence. The village on the other side of the river was alive with goats and horses and hens and

Heading for the canyon.

Camping by the river.

crowing roosters. I spoke Spanish to some local children who posed for a picture next to their favorite horse.

RAFTING THE RIVER AGAIN

Back in Texas I needed a river guide to take me through Santa Elena Canyon. In the abandoned mining town of Terlingua, Malcolm MacRoberts agreed to take me downriver in a rubber raft.

Heading for Santa Elena Canyon, we went twirling down the river under the brutal summer sun. Chihuahua, the largest of the Mexican states, was on our right. Texas was on our left. The river at this point was about forty yards wide. Aside from the excitement of a few rapids (the first one was called *Matadero*, the "Killer"), time stood absolutely still in the heat among the rocks. Around us were desert plants—the mesquite, the river willow, the prickly pear. Catfish and carp and the long-nose gar swam beneath the raft. Somewhere in the cliffs above us panthers roamed.

Large pesky yellow wasps dove for our food, while turkey vultures circled over the desert. Although migratory birds would return in the winter—tanagers, painted buntings, vermilion flycatchers, and cardinals—mostly we saw roadrunners speeding through the mesquite.

At one point the river became so narrow that Malcolm could put one oar on the United States and the other oar on Mexico. How, I wondered, would this river make it all the way to the Gulf! It still had hundreds of miles to go.

Malcolm MacRoberts.

After a long day on the Rio Grande, we camped at the entrance to Santa Elena Canyon. I set up my tent in a windstorm that blew dust into my eyes and nearly carried away the tent. Malcolm warned me that in July it can rain so furiously that all the water from the surrounding terrain finds its way to the Rio Grande and becomes a torrent. The river can rise twelve feet in an hour. So I was glad when Malcolm said he would sleep by the raft and watch the river closely.

That night the moon rose full over the rim of the high canyon wall. I could not sleep with the constant sound of the entrance rapids in my ears.

The next day the raft bounced back and forth off Mexico and Texas, the two rock walls of the canyon rising fifteen hundred feet above us. Sometimes the river, the international border, was only forty feet wide, then thirty-five, then, in a rock-strewn area called the "Rock Slide," the great Rio Grande was squeezed down to a width less than the raft, and we got stuck between the two countries.

Here the boulders were the size of houses blocking the river's passage. I pulled from the front of the raft while Malcolm buried himself in the rushing water. He crouched low and pushed the raft up with his shoulder. I pulled and nothing happened. Then pulled again. And slowly, slowly we inched the thousand-pound rubber beast onto its side and

The river squeezes through the "Rock Slide."

Navigating the canyon.

Stuck between two countries.

wiggled it back and forth over the boulder and into another small channel. And continued on.

With a slight wind in my face it didn't feel like 110 degrees. When I swam behind the raft, my feet touched bottom. Floating on the warm gentle current, looking up at thousands of feet of rock on both sides of the narrow brown river, my shouts echoed spookily off the walls. This was one of the finest memories I have of my trip. After two days of rafting I realized we had seen no one besides ourselves. My idea of time would never be the same after floating down this hot, timeless river.

Floating in the Rio Grande.

CHAPTER FOUR

◆　◆　◆

THE LOWER RIVER

A RIVER IN PERIL

As I approached the Gulf, the air grew dense and humid over the river like a wet sponge. I saw palm trees in this southernmost part of Texas. Cicadas pierced the sky. At the ferry at Ebanos, the only hand-pulled ferry on the river, I met an old man with white hair named Nieves, "Snow." He had worked on the ferry for forty-two years.

At Laredo I crossed the bridge into Nuevo Laredo. Then I drove miles and miles into the hot, dry land of Mexico to see an 18th-century ghost town. Founded in 1750, Guerrero Viejo had lost all eight thousand of its residents when the massive Falcon Dam on the Rio Grande formed a lake that flooded the town. For safety everyone had been moved off the river to Guerrero Nuevo.

41

The lone resident of Guerrero Viejo.

A herder drives his goats through the deserted streets.

When I reached the ghost town, a woman appeared like a ghost herself in the doorway of a crumbling old building. She said her name was Julia Samora. She spoke to me in Spanish. Born and raised here, Julia said she'd stayed behind for forty-five years since the dam had formed the lake in 1952. She'd had to move from house to house as the water rose. Even her children had moved to the new town. But she had not wanted to move, and I wondered what kind of life she lived being the only resident of a ghost town. Terribly lonely, I would think.

But this ghost town was in fact coming back from the dead. Mexico had had a long drought, and the lake had receded, and now the flooded buildings like the old church had recently, magically, re-emerged from the waters. Julia seemed proud of this fact. Sadly she knew also that no one would ever come back to the old town to live again.

As I approached the end of the river, thunderclouds were massing. Here at the southern tip of Texas is the most subtropical region of the Rio Grande. Palm forests had once stretched up the river for twenty miles. But now the unique plants of the region, like the Texas sabal palmetto and the ebony, have all but disappeared because of overdevelopment.

The lower Rio Grande Valley as seen from a Landsat satellite on April 22, 1997. This computer image was taken from approximately 500 miles above the earth. Mexico can be seen in the very lower portion of the image, Texas at the top. The blue area on the right is the Gulf of Mexico.

The United States Department of Agriculture monitors conditions in the valley by studying satellite imagery. Colors: green = vegetation; dark blue = water; white = sand; brown and red = bare soil.

If you look closely you can see a thin straight line, or "cut," in the lower right-hand corner of the image. This is a ship channel. Brownsville, Texas, lies to the left of the ship channel. Matamoros, Mexico, lies immediately south.

The lower Rio Grande Valley is perhaps the most imperiled ecosystem on the entire river. From 1900 to 1950 the region's population multiplied ten times. Sorghum, cotton, grapefruit, and sugar were cultivated. Factories, malls, and houses conquered the tropical forest. As great numbers of people pushed into the area around Brownsville and Matamoros, the river was controlled to prevent its unpredictable cycles of drought and flood. Levees and reservoirs were built. And the ecosystem of the river, in spite of attempts by conservationists, has never really recovered.

E P I L O G U E

◆　　　◆　　　◆

THE GULF OF MEXICO

Around Brownsville, there was so much development I literally lost the river. I could not find a road that would take me to the water. So I drove my car three miles along a beach to find the mouth of the Rio Grande. The mouth of the third longest river in the United States is so remote, few tourists ever see it.

My car almost got stuck in the deep sand. But I managed to drive along the water's edge, where the sand was harder.

When I reached the Rio Grande, I recognized it immediately. Here at the end of its journey it was no wider than it had been in Creede, almost two thousand miles upriver.

Sea gulls soared above. Sandpipers scampered on the sand where the little brown river was feeding fresh water into the briny vastness of the Gulf of Mexico. The sun blasted out of the clouds. All around me the surf and the sea wind sang their ancient songs.

Mexicans and Americans fished with nets and rods. There were fishermen on both sides of the Great River, as if no international border existed here, as if there were no reason whatsoever for keeping people apart.

I jumped into the sea to swim in the amazing Gulf, which turned azure green in the tropical sun. The salt on my skin reminded me that the river had now won its freedom where it met the wide sea.

I felt the joy of having followed a river from its source to its mouth. This long bony river had courageously traveled from the Continental Divide in the Colorado Rockies, past the silver mines of Creede, through many irrigated fields, to the Pueblo reservations, past the ancient petroglyphs of enchanted New Mexico, to El Paso, Texas. Then the river had braved a desert, struggled a thousand miles along the border, through Big Bend canyons a quarter-mile high, to the crowded lower valley. And finally here it was, the Rio Grande, flowing bravely into the Gulf of Mexico. The valiant river had run its grand course to the sea.

AUTHOR'S NOTE

Respecting the wishes of the Cochiti Pueblo, I have not included any photographs of their annual corn festival. Contemporary images of Pueblo ceremonies from time to time do appear in print but are often reproduced without the consent of the Pueblo.

The issue of immigration across the Rio Grande border is complex and sensitive. To do the topic justice requires greater study. I encourage my readers to visit their libraries and read further about the relations between Mexico and the United States.—P. L.

The author wishes to thank the following individuals for their help in the creation of this book: Diane Bird, Museum of Indian Arts & Culture, Museum of New Mexico; Joe Sando, Director of Archives, Pueblo Indian Cultural Center, Albuquerque, New Mexico; Arthur Olivas, Museum of New Mexico; Ed Hargraves, Creede Historical Society; Lorena Escobar, Mexican Mission to the United Nations; Doug Mosier, U. S. Border Patrol, Dept. of Justice; James H. Everett, U. S. Dept. of Agriculture, Integrated Farming in Natural Resources, Weslaco, Texas.

To learn more about rivers, contact RiverResource, an educational resource on the World Wide Web devoted to the rivers of the world: www.RiverResource.com

Additional photographs courtesy of:
Creede Historical Society: pp. 11, 13;
Library of Congress: pp. 12, 25, 32 (left);
Museum of New Mexico: pp. 19, 23, 25 (right);
Texas State Library & Archives: pp. 25 28, 30;

U. S. Dept. of Agriculture, Weslaco, TX: p 43.
Text and photographs copyright © 1999 by Peter Lourie
All rights reserved

Published by Caroline House
Boyds Mills Press, Inc.
A Highlights Company
815 Church Street
Honesdale, Pennsylvania 18431
Printed in the United States of America

Publisher Cataloging-in-Publication Data

Lourie, Peter
  Rio Grande : from the Rocky Mountains to the Gulf of Mexico / by Peter Lourie.—1st. ed.
[48]p. : col. ill. ; cm.
Summary: A photo essay about a journey along the Rio Grande, from the Rockies to the Gulf of Mexico.
ISBN 1-56397-706-0 hc   1-56397-896-2 pbk
1. Rio Grande Valley—Juvenile literature. 2. United States—Description and travel—Guidebooks—Juvenile literature. [1. Rio Grande Valley. 2. United States—Description and travel—Guidebooks.] I. Title
917.3—dc21 1999 AC CIP
Library of Congress Catalog Card Number 97-77907

First edition, 1999 / First Boyds Mills Press paperback edition, 2000
The text of this book is set in 13-point Minion

10 9 8 7 6 5 4 3 2 hc
10 9 8 7 6 5 4 3 2 1 pbk

Visit our website: www.boydsmillspress.com